ČESKÝ KRUMLOV

The Historical Section of the Town, the Castle and the Château

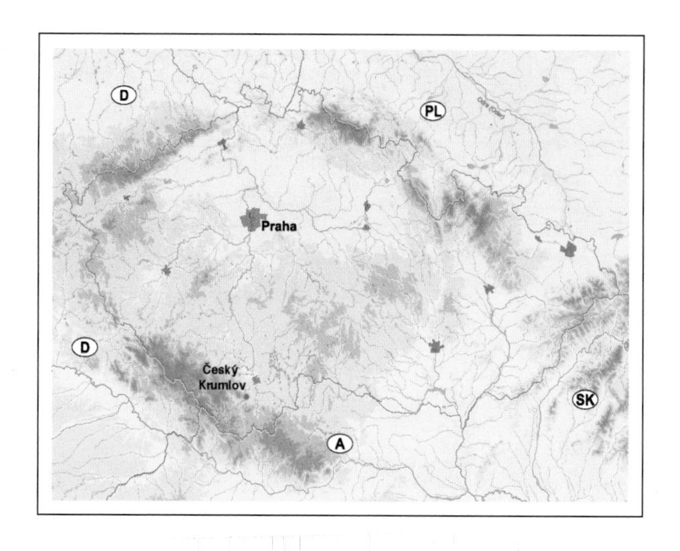

Welcome to Český Krumlov. The town's exceptional atmosphere and in particular its unique historical monuments make Český Krumlov a true jewel among the towns and cities of the Czech Republic. It includes the most extensive complex of castle and château structures in Bohemia, which throughout the town's colourful past has served as the residence of some of the most powerful aristocratic houses in the land. The Latrán and Old Town (Staré město) sections of the town include many stone burghers' houses, which have preserved their medieval and Renaissance character and around which a number of august sacred structures have been erected. In 1992, this remarkable historical unit was entered into the UNESCO list of world cultural and natural heritage and it is one of the most visited locations in the Czech Republic. In this publication, we hope to provide you with a basic overview of the history of the town and to introduce you to selected monuments both in the town's suburbs and in the château complex. We hope that the following pages will provide you with an integrated overview of Český Krumlov, which will help you to find your way around the town, introduce you to a wide variety of interesting sights or remind you in the future of the pleasant times you spent here.

The editors

Materials published by and consultations with the following historians, art-historians, monument protection workers, archivists, and researchers were drawn upon: Bloch J., Bůžek V., Cichrová K., Dvořák F., Horyna M., Hrubeš K. , Jakab M., Jelínek P., Korychová M., Kubíková A., Lancinger J., Mašková V., Mencl V., Muk J., Müller J., Olšan J., Pavelec P., Slavko P., Slavková S., Stejskal A., Záloha J., etc., and the Official Information System of the Český Krumlov region – www.ckrumlov.cz – was used when compiling this guide.

ČESKÝ KRUMLOV
The Historical Section of the Town, the Castle and the Château

Publisher: Unios CB, spol. s r. o.
MCU vydavatelství Unios, Hany Kvapilové 10, 370 10 České Budějovice,
Tel./Fax: +420/387 428 360, e-mail: vydavatelstvi@unios.cz, www.unios.cz
Technical editors: Pavel Dvořák, Radek Eliášek, Petr Steinbauer
Text: Mgr. Zdena Flašková
Photographs: Libor Sváček
Maps: SHOCart Zlín
Commercial presentation: MCU vydavatelství Unios, Marek Otípka
Typesetting: Jan Kubeš
Printing: Typodesign, s. r. o., České Budějovice
Distribution: GeoClub s. r. o., www.geoclub.cz,
Prague – tel.: +420/283 890 152, fax: +420/283 890 153, e-mail: praha@geoclub.cz
Brno – tel.: +420/545 229 343, fax: +420/545 229 345, e-mail: brno@geoclub.cz

1st edition, České Budějovice 2002
4th publication in the Uniosguide series, 64 pages

ISBN 80-86141-35-7
ISBN 80-86141-36-5 (angl. vyd.)

A view from the Mountain of the Cross (Křížová hora) with Kleť (1084 m) in the background

THE HISTORY OF THE TOWN

This locality was endowed from the beginning of time with a certain attraction as a place suitable for a settlement. During the Bronze Age a trade route led along the Vltava valley. The top of the hill overlooking the river offered a position of strategic importance. The oldest proof of the existence of an early settlement here is evidently a stone axe-like weapon dating back to around 4000 years BC, which was found by chance in the 1st courtyard of the château. Archaeological research in parts of the 2nd courtyard in 1994-1995 uncovered finds indicating that a settlement existed here in about 1500 BC during the early Bronze Age. A small collection of pottery proves the existence of a settlement probably located on a rise, maybe a fortified settlement. Other fragments of pottery are evidence of a late Hallstatt settlement around 500 BC and a late La Téne settlement roughly 150 years BC.

The beginnings of a **medieval settlement** are substantiated also only by archaeological finds. The earliest written mention of Český Krumlov castle is apparently that contained in the poem "Der Frauendienst", written by the Austrian cavalier-minstrel Ulrich von Liechtenstein in 1240-1242. The first written report explicitly mentioning the existence of a place called "Chrumbenowe", meaning Krumlov, dates from 1253. The Latin name "castrum Crumnau" or the old-German "Crumbenowe" actually refer to the place where the castle stood. "Krumme Aue" means "crooked-shaped meadow", a place located on a crooked-shaped meadow or lea, and this actually corresponds with

The fresco of the Rožmberk Rider (Latrán 39)

the shape of the town at that time, which was encircled by the snake-like meandering of the River Vltava.

Preserved written sources tell us of the **noble families** that chose Český Krumlov castle and château as their residence. We learn first about the Lords of Krumlov, who followed the powerful Czech House of Vitkovec nobles and at some time before 1250 founded the oldest Gothic castle at the locality of the present-day Little Castle (Hrádek) with a tower. Their coat-of-arms was a five-petalled rose, which also appears on the coat-of-arms of the Rožmberks, who gained the castle when the family of the Lords of Krumlov died out in 1302.

The Rožmberk family and their red five-petalled rose immediately spring to mind when Český Krumlov is mentioned. They resided here till 1602, longer than any other noble family. Members of the family belonged to the highest aristocratic circles, were clever managers, politicians and educated, cultured patrons of the fine arts. They gave the château its Renaissance style and changed it into a splendid noble residence. The last members of that famous family were the brothers William (1535-1592) and Petr Vok of Rožmberk (1539-1611). Petr Vok in particular is one of the best-known figures in Czech history. His wide interest in culture, his art collections and activities and life style, typical of the nobility in the Renaissance period, have often been portrayed in literature and films. The renovation of the château and town buildings in the Renaissance style was, however, mainly the work of William of Rožmberk.

In 1602 the Český Krumlov estate passed into the hands of **Rudolf II Habsburg**. His son, Don Julius d'Austria, who was illegitimate and quite insane, lived here from 1605 to 1608. He went down in history as the savage murderer of Markéta Pichler, the daughter of the local barber.

In 1622 Emperor Ferdinand II Habsburg gave the Krumlov Estate to the Steiermark **House of Eggenberg**. Three generations of this noble family lived here from 1622 to 1719. Their most notable member was the Krumlov duke, Jan Kristián of Eggenberg, a cultured and travelled cavalier who was well acquainted with the cultural standard of life at most of the European courts and towns of that period. During his life the château was a busy nob-

The atmosphere of a medieval town during the Celebration of the Five-Petalled Rose

le residence where cultural and social events were held, such as performances of plays, concerts, dances, masked balls and hunts, which were attended by many prominent guests and added to the general impression of a luxurious residence. The duke was a great lover of the arts, especially of music, operas and ballet, so it is not surprising to learn that the unique baroque theatre in the 5th courtyard was built during his time.

After 1719 the **House of Schwarzenberg** inherited the Krumlov estate and the château remained in the hands of that family of noble German extraction until 1947. They were efficient managers, politicians and successful courtiers, belonging to the highest noble circles, whose careers and personal lives were closely bound up with the Habsburg imperial court in Vienna. And it was that milieu that exerted such strong influence on Duke Josef Adam of Schwarzenberg and inspired him to undertake extensive renovations in the rococo style at the château. During that time a whole host of artists of good repute and renown in Europe gave the château, its halls and rooms as well as the château gardens more or less the appearance they have today.

The changes made in the second half of the 18th century under Josef Adam of Schwarzenberg were the last of any great significance to be made at the château. The following generations of the family gradually lost interest in making any large in-

An aerial view of the historical centre

vestments in the Český Krumlov residence, particularly after 1860 when they began to devote their time and activities to the Hluboká château in South Bohemia.

The Krumlov château was not even used regularly as a residence in the **20th century**. Nevertheless the Schwarzenbergs were well aware of its artistic and historical value. One proof of this is the series of renovation activities that began at the close of the 19th century in order to preserve the rare frescoes in the château courtyards and in the bowers. The last noble owner of the château was Adolf Schwarzenberg, who was a lawyer.

In 1947 the château was transferred as part of the Schwarzenberg property under Czech provincial ownership, and after this system was abolished it became the property of the state in 1949. At the present time the Český Krumlov castle and château are administered by the State Institution for the Care of Ancient Monuments in České Budějovice. The buildings, rooms and the château gardens are being successively restored, repaired and conserved, and all this work is always done with an eye to the historical sources, to ensure as much as possible that the original historical appearance of those parts is preserved or restored.

Today this enormous complex, created throughout the ages, constitutes an outstanding ancient monument. The Český Krumlov château has become an integral part of the cultural heritage not only of the people of the town, South Bohemia and the Czech Republic, but it has also become known to the public world-wide. Proof of its

The Budějovice Gate

The connecting passage

importance is the fact that the entire area containing the château was declared a **national cultural monument** in 1989, and in 1992 the entire historical complex was entered into the **UNESCO** list of world cultural and natural heritage.

THE HISTORICAL CENTRE

Visitors to Český Krumlov may come by many different routes and using various means of transport, but the lion's share of the million tourists that the town receives each year come along the road leading from České Budějovice. Local roads leading to the town centre branch off this road and visitors can enter the town, for example, via the **Budějovice Gate** (**Budějovická brána**). Český Krumlov originally had ten town gates, which formed an important part of the town's defences. However, most of the gates were demolished in the 19th century in connection with the development of transport and industry and today only one gate – the Budějovice Gate – remains. Despite its venerable age of 400 years, it was the youngest of the Krumlov gates built by Dominic Benedetto Cometta of Eckthurn in 1598 – 1602. The gate leads visitors to the oldest street in Český Krumlov and also to the town suburb of **Latrán**. The street takes you to the town centre and to the château. Just in front of the small square leading to the Red Gate (Červená brána), which is the main entry into the château complex, Latránská Street is spanned by a connecting passage in the

The monastery of the Order of the Knights of the Cross with the Red Star (formerly Minorite)

form of a characteristic "memorial arch" decorated with painted symbols in laurel wreathes and illusive bossage – a memorial to the House of Rožmberk. The symbols represent William of Rožmberk and his third wife Anna Marie of Baden.

The connecting passage is a unique system of mutually connected covered bridges and corridors, which was established under the last lord of the House of Rožmberk, developed under the House of Eggenberg and completed in the 18th century under the House of Schwarzenberg. Today, it forms the "backbone" of the Krumlov château, as all its buildings and palace structures are connected in this audacious arch. It arches from the château gardens over five château courtyards and mirrors the declining terrain down to the one-time Minorite and Poor Clare cloister and the widow's residence of Anna of Rogendorf. The overall length of this structure, which at one time had three storeys, is almost 1 km.

The current **monastery of the Order of the Knights of the Cross with the Red Star** was established in the former Poor Clare and Minorite cloister, which was founded in the 2nd half of the 14th century by the wife and sons of Petr I of Rožmberk. The present expansive complex of la-

The new apothecary

te Gothic and baroque buildings housed the Minorite monastery, the Poor Clare convent and the Convent of Godly Women.

The core of the Minorite monastery is the late Gothic cloister dating from around 1500 and vaulted with a tracery vault. The late Gothic Chapel of Saint Wolfgang dating from 1491 is a significant monument with its wall murals of scenes from the legend of St. Wolfgang, which was painted by V. Tschöpper in 1781. In the centre of the paradise garden stands the early baroque Chapel of the Virgin Mary of Einsiedeln dating from 1686 with a statue of the Black Mother of God.

If you return to the main Latrán street from the monastery, you pass by **house number 53**. The blind arcades on the façade of this house are decorated with alchemistic and cabalistic symbols, which come from the group of alchemists that lived in the court of William of Rožmberk. The arcades along the front façade bear a cycle of Renaissance paintings depicting the ten phases of the life of a man – from early childhood through to late old age and death. The paintings were apparently created some time around 1589.

Latrán number 39

The opposite **house number 46** is also called the **"New Apothecary" (Nová lékárna)**. The house's facing walls date from the Renaissance with sgraffito structuring from 1556 and they terminate in an attic gable. The western section of the building passes through the former connecting passage leading from the château to the Minorite monastery and the passage further continues along a floor in the neighbouring Red Gate (Červená brána). This house was originally home to the Rožmberk servants and later it served as the doctor's residence. In 1913, the ground floor was adapted to become the château apothecary and it continued to fulfil this function up to the 1950s.

Latrán number 15, the former home of the Rožmberk court painter, **Gabriel de Blonde**, is another interesting building. Its richly decorated Renaissance façade has survived to this day and inside there are murals depicting the Czech Patron Saints, Wenceslas (Václav), Vitas (Vít), Adalbert (Vojtěch), Sigmund (Zikmund), Prokop and Ludmila. This building is one of the most remarkable burgher's houses in the town, with a high degree of authenticity and only a few modern repairs.

Latrán number 37 is the former home of the Rožmberk courtier, Jetřich Slatinský of Slatinka, who lived there in the 16th century. The house's upper floor is supported by stone cantilevers, and the quoin stones, which the burghers used to protect the corners of their houses from the wheels of pas-

Houses in Latrán with the tower of the former Church of St. Jošt

The entrance to the château steps

sing carriages, are also of interest. The Café Fink, a favourite haunt of the expressionist Egon Schiele, was located there at the beginning of the 20th century.

If you turn left at this house, you can see the so-called **New Town** (**Nové město**). Sites of interest include, for example, the **brewery** buildings, which are the oldest part of the **widow's residence of Anna of Rogendorf** dating from the mid 16th century. The widow's residence also included a Renaissance garden. In the vicinity of the residence lies a small square known as **the Square at the Gate** (**Na fortně**) where the **Studio for International Ceramic Creations** (**Ateliér mezinárodní keramické tvorby**) is based.

From the Square at the Gate, you can then return to Latrán. The one-time **Church of Saint Jošt** (building number 6) was established at the beginning of the 14th century by Petr I of Rožmberk along with the Rožmberk hospital and poorhouse. Under the reforms of Josef II, the church was secularised and it was later sold in 1790 to a Krumlov burgher on the

The view across the river to the New Town

The Barber's Bridge (Lazebnický most) and the former barber's shop and Church of St. Jošt

The bailey

condition that he preserve the church spire, as public opinion at the time was that it beautified the town. The church and later the hospital were converted into flats, but the church spire still remains in place in accordance with the ancient wishes of the townsfolk.

Opposite the former church stands **Latrán number 1**, which used to be the barber's shop. The bridge across the River Vltava connecting this section of Latrán with the inner town recalls the use of this building in its name – it is known as the Barber's Bridge (Lazebnický most). The barber's shop is mentioned in the town's franchise dating from 1347. The house was built during the Gothic period and it was originally built up to the town fortifications and the former gate. The barber's services were a part of the inherent "local colour" of the town from as early as the Middle Ages.

The wooden **Barber's Bridge (Lazebnický most)** across the River Vltava connects Latrán with the former Old Town (Staré město). Today, there are statues dating from the 19th century along the sides of the bridge. Along the right-hand side, they depict the crucified Christ and along the left-hand side they depict Saint John of Nepomuk, the patron saint of the bridge.

On the other side of the bridge on the left-hand side, you can see **Parkán Street** (Bailey street), the name of which was first mentioned in 1443. Its name is derived from the former town fortifications, known as "parkán" (baileys), which led from the Barber's Bridge along the River Vltava to

Wide Street (Široká ulice)

the former mill, which stood below the site of the current museum. Bailey Street consists of the houses of small tradesmen, which were mainly built in the space between two ramparts. The balcony corridors of these houses above the River Vltava contribute to the typical character of the town's built-up areas.

Parkán Street is now full of small guesthouses and stylised inns, which offer the opportunity to sit in pleasant historical interiors and in the forecourt gardens on the banks of the River Vltava. A typical example of this is **Krčma u Dwau Maryí** (house number 104), the walls of which contain part of the medieval bailey ramparts, a scullery, a beam-and-plank floor and two wall murals of the Virgin Mary of Mariazell on the front façade of the building. The refreshments served in this tavern are also stylised and they revive the tastes that could be found on the tables of the burghers of years long passed.

The central **Town Hall Street** (**Radniční ulice**) was known as Cheese Street (Sýrová ulice) in the 18th century. It is directly connected with the Barber's Bridge and leads around the quoin of the town

Fisherman Street (Rybářská ulice) on the left-hand bank of the Vltava

The former town brewery, now the Egon Schiele Art Centre

hall directly onto the square. Walk along the street up to house number 29 and turn right onto Long Street (Dlouhá ulice). Precious Gothic wall murals were discovered in this house in 2001 and restored by the artist Karl Hrubeš.

These are clearly **the oldest Gothic murals in Český Krumlov** and they date from the 2nd half of the 14th century. The preserved fragment includes an expansive figural composition framed with painted Gothic architecture and a decorated with acanthus leaves. The paintings were discovered by chance during restoration work carried out on the building. Together with the paintings discovered at house number 1 on the Square of Concord (Náměstí Svornosti), this represents one of the most significant finds of Gothic painting to be realised at the turn of the 20th and 21st centuries.

Long Street (Dlouhá ulice) leads into Wide Street (Široká ulice) and it is formed by rows of mainly Gothic-Renaissance houses with baroque or classicist elements. The Rožmberk regent, Jakub Krčín of Jelčany, and the Rožmberk court painter, Bartholomew Beránek-Jelínek (the artist responsible for the painted decorations on the tower of the Krumlov château) lived in the house at number 32 in the 16th century.

In the 16th – 17th centuries, Wide Street (Široká ulice) was called Rear (Zadní) or Lower (Dolní) Street and it was the widest street in the town, meaning that regular markets were held there. By turning right into Wide Street from Long Street, you pass the building of the former **town armoury** (house number 86) up to the so-called **Island (Ostrov)**, from where there is an impressive view of the cambered structures of the château architecture of the main palace buildings, the "Clad Bridge" (Plášťový most) and the château theatre.

However, by turning left, you pass **house number 77**, which was owned in the 16th century by the manager of the Rožmberk Mine and the renowned alchemist, Antonín Michael of Ebbersbach.

The dominant building in Wide Street (Široká ulice) is the expansive structure of the former **town brewery** (numbered 70 and 71), which was built according to a Renaissance design of the Italian architect, Dominic Benedetto Cometta of Eckthurn, on the site of four medieval houses. The brewery underwent several renovations and in the 1870s several industrial buildings and a cold store were added to it. The brewery ceased its operations in the mid 20th century as a result of World War II. Nowadays, the **Egon Schiele Art Centre** is located within the brewery facility.

By passing the corner house at **number 54** with its preserved Renaissance paintwork with a predominance of ornamental decorations, figural motifs (St. James, St. Philip and St. Florien and fictive portraits of men, woman and an ape), illusive architectural elements and caryatides, you come to the Little Square at the Pool (náměstíčko Na Louži). This house belongs is one of the most interesting monuments in the historical centre. The painted decorations on the façade were without doubt undertaken by the same painting workshop as that which worked on the château for William of Rožmberk.

The corner of Town Hall Street (Radniční ulice) and Long Street (Dlouhá ulice)

Corner house number 54 with its preserved Renaissance paintings

If you head straight along **Kájovská Street** in the direction of the River Vltava, you can view the remains of the former town fortifications on the right-hand side and then on the left-hand side the former **paper mill (papírna)** (building number 56) before you arrive at the **Dr. Eduard Beneš Bridge (most Dr. Edwarda Beneše)**. **Fisherman Street (Rybářská ulice)**, one of the oldest streets in Český Krumlov, begins on the other side of the bridge and it still has the character of a unilaterally developed embankment. To the left of the bridge lies the **Town Park (Městský park)** with its former **Jesuit summer residence** (today building number 55 – the Bohemia Gold Hotel) and the Chapel of St. Martin, which used to be surrounded by a cemetery.

By returning to the Little Square at the Pool to the right, you pass building **number 12** on Krumlov's square. This building is currently part of a hotel and its southern façade, around which you can walk, is divided by two late Gothic bay windows with three cantilevers. Both of the central cantilevers are decorated with the symbol of the five-petalled rose of the Rožmberks.

The Square of Concord (Náměstí Svornosti) forms the centre of the former Old Town. This part of the town was established using a regular colonisation ground plan typical for the 13th century with a right-angled square in the middle and

The Square of Concord (Náměstí Svornosti) with the frontages of the burghers' houses

a connecting network of streets, which bordered individual blocks of houses and are connected with the town gates and ramparts of the day. The surface of the square slopes gradually downwards towards the River Vltava.

The town-planning layout of the Old Town was naturally limited by the meanderings of the River Vltava, which flows around the town's outer edge and thus forms its natural boundary. The bend in the river begins in the place where the former so-called Upper Gate (Horní brána) once stood and the river then flows around the Old Town on the right-hand bank and the château, Latrán and the New Town on the left-hand bank, whereby an elegant curve enables it to return once again to the very beginning of the bend, to a place known as the Mouse Hole (Myší díra). The well-known **Rumyší díra** tavern and river bath have stood at this important site since time immemorial.

The square is defined by four rows of burghers' houses, the bulk of which are mainly Gothic or Renaissance. The façades of these houses are mostly interconnected with arcades. The houses were originally mostly wooden, while the stone structures on Krumlov's square were mainly established in the 14th and 15th centuries.

The **Town Hall** located at **building number 1 on the square** was established by means of the gradual connection of two originally Gothic houses. This involved a typical Renaissance method of combining two narrow Gothic buildings into a single magnificent Renaissance structure. The buildings were probably connected some time around the year 1597 and the building was given a unifying Renaissance escutcheon, which was simplified in 1796 into

The Town Hall

a classicist attic gable. The attic gable is decorated with two fascias of parapet stones and balusters and with rococo vases made of baked clay. The front façade of the building is decorated with the following symbols: the symbol of the town of Český Krumlov, the symbol of the Bohemian lands and the coats of arms of the Houses of Eggenberg and Schwarzenberg. The significant Gothic and Renaissance architectural components (arches, portals, window jambs ...) and in particular the late Gothic murals from the first half of the 15th century are worthy of mention. A mural can be seen in the entrance area of the present Museum of Torture (Muzeum útrpného práva) and it depicts a fragment from the scene of the adoration of the three wise men.

The stones of the expansive cellars of this building, which today serve as an exhibition area in the above-mentioned museum, also offer a very impressive insight into medieval vaulting.

However, prior to 1519 the original town hall was located in **building number 3.** The initial development of the building lot occurred during the establishment of the town of Český Krumlov and it stretched back to the period around 1300. It is clear that the oldest provable Český Krumlov town hall was established in this building after the Hussite Wars.

On the right-hand side a narrow alley leads along this house to the former **town lock-up** (building n. 143), which was originally part of the town hall. After 1519, when the town hall was relocated to its present position, the town kept the lock-up and it continued to function until the 18th century.

The dominant feature of the square today is without doubt the fountain and the plague pillar. **The plague pillar** with its statue of the Immaculate Virgin Mary is the work of the Prague sculptor Matyáš Václav Jäckel and the local stonemason, Jan Plansker, dating from 1712-1716. The column is now part of the fountain and it is decorated with statues of the patron saints and the protectors against plague infections: St. Wenceslas (Václav), St. Vitas (Vít), St. John the Evangelist (Jan Evangelista) and St. Jude Thaddeus (Juda Tadeáš) in the upper row and St. Francis Xavier (František Xaverský), St. Sebastian (Šebestián), St. Gaetano (Kajetán) and St. Rochus (Roch) in the lower row. The construction of the column was financed by Marie Ernestina of Schwarzenberg and it was an expression of gratitude to the holy protectors for concluding the plague epidemic, which rocked the town in 1680-1682.

An integral part of the column today is the **fountain**, which was however transferred to this site in 1844 as a result of the growing traffic requirements in the town.

From the square, you can head upwards along **Upper Street (Horní ulice)** in the

The château and the area under the château – the New Town and Latrán

The complex of the former Jesuit hostel, now the Hotel Růže (Rose Hotel)

direction of the Church of Saint Vitas (kostel sv. Víta). Almost half of Upper Street consists of buildings that in the past were owned by the church, and in some cases this is still the case. These include the former chaplain's house, the church, the expansive prelate's palace, the Jesuit seminary and the Jesuit theatre and hostel. Most of these buildings were interconnected and it was possible to walk from one to the other while remaining indoors – this offers the opportunity of comparison with the château's connecting passage. This part of the town can be said to be a sort of antipole to the expansive Krumlov château facility, which was a seat of worldly power. Just as the château area is spread out on a cliff overlooking the Vltava and its spire forms a significant dominant feature of the landscape, the buildings subject to ecclesiastical power are spread out on a cliff on the other side of the river, dominated by the neo-Gothic spire of the Church of Saint Vitas. The houses of the inhabitants of Český Krumlov both symbolically and physically sit below these powers in the "valley".

When approaching the church steps along the right-hand side of Upper Street (Horní ulice), you can see a superb architectural monument located at building number 159, the so-called **Kaplanka**. This late Gothic building contains the first entry of the Renaissance style into Český Krumlov. A significant feature of the main façade is the right-angled bartizan, which is buttressed with a semi-column decorated with spiral fluting. The symbol of the five-petalled rose of Rožmberk appears under the stone windowsill on the bartizan.

Building number 162, the oldest school in Český Krumlov, lies to the right of the Church of Saint Vitas. The parish school was established as early as at the beginning of the 15th century.

The construction of the Parish **Church of St. Vitas** (farní kostel sv. Víta) began in 1407 according to a design by Linhart of Aldenberg at the instigation of the pastor, Hostislav of Bílsko. The monumental Gothic structure was built on the site of the original smaller church, which had become too small to accommodate the growing number of inhabitants in the town. The church was consecrated in 1439 and it was surrounded by a cemetery up to 1585, a fact that is borne out by the several gravestones still in place today. In 1593 – 97, the church interior was enriched with a monumental tomb with the epitaph of William of Rožmberk. In 1638, the new sacristy was built, in 1726 – 29 the Chapel of St. John of Nepomuk (kaple sv. Jana Nepomuckého) was added and in 1893 – 94 the original church spire with the cupola was replaced with today's thin neo-Gothic spire.

There is a mural of the Assumption of the Virgin Mary dating from the 15th century above the entrance portal. The interior of the church includes a triple nave, a vaulted chancel, a tracery vault in the main nave and cross-arched vaulting in the side naves. The vault in the central nave is painted with the coat of arms of Linhart of Aldenberg. **The main altar** with its depic-

The picturesque roofs and escutcheons of the houses in the oldest part of the Old Town

tion of the patrons of the church (St. Vitas and the Virgin Mary) dates from 1683 and it was donated to the church by the ruling lordly couple of the time, a fact which is still commemorated on the altar by the alliance mark of Jan Kristián of Eggenberg and Marie Ernestina, nee of Schwarzenberg. The altarpiece was painted over in 1897. The neo-gothic side altar also comes from the same period.

The left-hand, northern wall of the side nave is decorated with murals dating from the mid 15th century and depicting several saints (St. Agnes (Anežka), St. Catherine (Kateřina)) and scenes from the crucifixion. The entrance into the Chapel of St. John of Nepomuk is located next to these scenes. The marble relief panels from the **gravestone of William of Rožmberk** and his third wife, Anna Marie of Rožmberk (nee of Baden) are located in this chapel.

The Chapel of St. John of Nepomuk (kaple sv. Jana Nepomuckého) was established by a different aristocratic couple: Duke Adam František of Schwarzenberg and his wife Eleanor Amelie of Schwarzenberg, nee of Lobkowice. The chapel was built by E. A. Martinelli and the hearts of its founders are buried there. The chapel altar includes a painting of the death of John of Nepomuk dating from 1729 and painted by Pietro van Roy.

The main altar in the Church of St. Vitas

A further area is the originally Gothic and later baroque renovated **Chapel of the Resurrection** (kaple Vzkříšení), in which František Jakub Prokyš did the rococo paintings in 1777.

A beautiful small baroque organ dating from 1716 is situated in the side gallery above the entrance into the church. The organ is decorated with carved and gold-plated motifs of acanthus leaves.

The western, late **Gothic gallery** is the work of the Rožmberk construction works and it was built around 1500 for the local **literary brotherhood**. This brotherhood was a guild of educated burghers, who sang in the church on Sundays and during special morning masses.

Building number 155, the former **prelate's palace**, is also connected to the Parish Church of St. Vitas. This originally Gothic structure dating from the 14th century underwent several bouts of reconstruction work, of which the most significant gave rise to the rococo cloisters in the inner courtyard dating from 1769. The main neo-Renaissance façade, dating from the 19th century, faces Upper Street (Horní ulice) and it is divided into three sections. Its walls are covered in sgraffito with the rosette motif, and the frontage with the date 1576 has been completed with historical escutcheons with classical decorative elements. The main façade includes a memorial plaque to the prelate Jiří Bílek of Bílenberk (1588 – 1657). The interior of the prelate's palace is graced with the ceremo-

The Church of St. Vitas

The Jesuit seminary (Museum)

nial **"Prokyš's Hall" (Prokyšův sál)**, which was decorated with a rococo illusive painting by František Jakub Prokyš in 1769.

The neighbouring **building number 154**, the present Hotel Růže (Rose Hotel), was built in 1586 – 90 at the instigation of William of Rožmberk on the site of several demolished Gothic houses. It was one of the very first Jesuit hostels in Bohemia and it was built according to a design of the architect Baldassare Maggi of Arogno.

The keys to the hostel were ceremonially handed over to the rector of the Prague Jesuit Hostel, Alexander Vojta, in the hostel courtyard in 1588 by William of Rožmberk. The building's ground floor was designated for the students, while the next floor was for the Jesuits. The building also included a chapel. Students gathered in the hostel from all over south Bohemia, especially in order to learn German. One of the most significant Jesuits to stay at the hostel for a while was Bohuslav Balbín. The Jesuits remained there until the dissolution of the order in 1773. The building began to be used as a hotel in 1889 and it was ceremonially named the "Rose".

This expansive two-storeyed Renaissance building has four wings built around a central rectangular courtyard. The building's façades are decorated with sgraffito and wall murals in lunette cornices and the walls of the inner courtyards include the IHS symbol of the Jesuit order, the coat of arms of the founders of the hostel (William of Rožmberk and his fourth wife Polyxena of Rožmberk, nee of Pernštejn) and a depiction of the Rožmberk rider. The rear façade facing the River Vltava is once again decorated with a lunette cornice and with a richly painted solar clock.

The contemporary Hotel Růže also includes **building number 153**. From the beginning of the 16th century, this building was home to the Tancl family, who were butchers. The painted coat of arms of the Guild of Butchers (two crossed axes on a yellow field under the Rožmberk five-petalled rose) on the building's façade serves as a reminder of this fact. In 1590, the town council purchased the house at the wish of William of Rožmberk and presented it to the Jesuits as a gift. In 1613, the Jesuits established there the first ever theatre equipped with wooden machinery for the fast changing of scenery. This theatre has been renovated several times in recent years.

Drama was part of the Jesuits' training and college semesters often ended with a theatre production in Latin, in which the local students acted. **The Jesuit performances** made use of themes from church history, biblical topics or tales, which were strongly emotional, religious and morally uplifting.

The opposite house at number 152 was the former **Jesuit seminary**, which con-

A bird's eye view of the château complex

The majestic residence of important aristocratic families

cludes the expansive complex of ecclesiastical buildings in Upper Street (Horní ulice). The structure stands alone on a rocky ridge above a trenched isthmus at the narrowest point of the bend of the River Vltava. It was the first early baroque building built in the town in 1650 – 1652 by A. P. Golsts on the site of six Gothic burghers' houses. From the time of its establishment, the building fulfilled educational requirements until 1946, when it became the home of the collections and exhibits of the District Museum (Okresní museum).

The Upper Gate (Horní brána) once stood between today's District National History Museum (Okresní vlastivědné museum) and the Hotel Růže. It was used to guard the southern entry into the town. It was 32 m high, making it the highest of the Krumlov gates, and the first mention of it was made in 1497. Originally, access to the gate was via a wooden drawbridge, but this was later replaced with a stone bridge at the end of the 18th century. The Upper Gate was the first of all the gates to be demolished in 1839 and today the only reminder of its existence is the name of the adjacent town suburb.

The site of the no longer existing Upper Gate serves as our exit point from the historical core of Český Krumlov. If you have time or the appetite, you can take a walk in the surroundings and climb, for example, up to the chapel on the **Mountain of the Cross** (kaple na Křížové hoře). From there, you can see a wonderful view of the town stretching up to the green frame of the Blanský Forest (Blanský les) crowned

The northern side of the palace buildings

with the silhouette of **Mount Kleť**. For many inhabitants of South Bohemia, the panorama of Český Krumlov and Kleť with its television transmission tower are just as powerful symbols of home as the panorama of Prague Castle above the Vltava is for all inhabitants of Bohemia. The irreplaceable character of this countryside and the architecture integrated into it makes this place a rare "cultural and natural heritage", which not only the world community represented by UNESCO, but also every inhabitant of Krumlov, South Bohemia and Bohemia itself can appreciate and protect as part of their personal pride and national identity.

THE CASTLE AND THE CHÂTEAU

The Český Krumlov castle and château combine to form one of the most priceless historical monuments in the Czech Republic. This is not only due to the number of mainly Gothic, Renaissance and Baroque structures as a whole, but also due to all

The 1st internal courtyard – the salt-house building on the left, the former hippodrome on the right

the individual parts and details. Among the rare features we can mention the frescoes and graffiti decorating the façades, the sculptural works in the grounds, remarkably decorated halls, ornamented wood ceilings and wooden inlaid floors, furniture, the unique wooden mechanism of the theatre, the remarkably designed vaults, different types of trusses, gables, portals and jambs, stucco ornamentation and so on. A wealth of forms and styles can be seen e. g. in the many chimneys – with only one exception there are not two chimneys the same to be found on the château buildings.

William of Rožmberk, Jan Kristián of Eggenberg, Josef Adam of Schwarzenberg

The complex of castle and château buildings, the second largest of its kind in the Czech Republic, was built on high rocks overlooking the valley of the River Vltava. Today this area contains nearly 40 buildings of the medieval castle and the newly fashioned château together with eleven hectares of château gardens, which gradually merge into the countryside. The palatial buildings and other structures dominated by the Český Krumlov round tower have been looking down for centuries from the hill onto the cluster of little town houses below the château. Throughout the ages life at the château has been inseparably joined to that of the town.

Sightseeing tours of the château and its grounds are a great attraction and experience. Every day and night, at every time of the year, the château radiates a distinct atmosphere and creates a specific mood among the many visitors during their tour. There are several ways to the château but the most usual is the tour beginning at the **1st courtyard**.

That courtyard was once the farming area of the castle, where the servants and artisans lived and the farm animals were kept. It can be entered from three sides: through a small gateway leading from the Jelení Gardens, through the big Red Gate (Červená brána) leading from the main street in the town centre (Latrán) or via the château steps, which follow the line of the old path going down to the former ford on the Vltava River where the Barber's Bridge (Lazebnický most) now stands.The 1st courtyard was formerly called the Animal Run **(Rejdiště)** and was an enclosure where the farm animals ran freely around and drank from the well there. The Animal Run was abolished in 1853 on the orders of Jan Adolf II of Schwarzenberg and a garden was laid out here around the fountain, thus forming a pleasant oasis of peace not far from the busy main path through the château grounds.

The buildings in the 1st courtyard served economic and administrative purposes. Their architecture went through several changes of style over the centuries. Some of the Gothic structures were gradually adapted into Renaissance, then Baroque and Classicist styles, and this was continued in some cases in the 19th and 20th centuries, according to the purposes for which the structures were used. The Gothic **Salt-house (Solnice)** at **No. 57** for example, which stands to the right of the Red Gate was first a malt-house, then a granary, and finally it became a salt-house, hence its present name. Today it houses several firms, an Internet café and a Tourist Information Centre.

House No. 46 with Renaissance graffiti on the façade, which stands left of the Red Gate, has also gone through changes over the years. It was first a dwelling for the Rožmberk courtiers and cavaliers, from the 17th to 19th centuries it was the residence of the manorial physician and from 1915 onwards it was the manorial pharmacy. In the neighbouring building **(No. 232)** there were stables and granaries. It also underwent changes; in the 20th century it was used by the local Nazi organisation NSDAP, then later as the administration centre of the estate and from the 1950s as the headquarters of the local Public Security Force. Today it is used for exhibitions in the so-called Columned Hall (Sloupová síň).

If we go through the little park round the fountain to the refreshment kiosk, we come to the former icehouse and smithy. The two-storeyed Renaissance building **No. 65** with graffiti and a sundial dating from 1690 decorating the facade was once a very important building; it was a **brewery** that the former Rožmberk regent, Jakub Krčín of Jelčany had completed in 1579. It functioned till 1623. Attached to it is a row of one-storeyed cottages that were used by artisans as workshops. At the end of the row we come to the two-storeyed former **manorial hospice** (No. 184), on the first floor of which a manorial hospital existed from 1775.

Coats of arms of William of Rožmberk, Jan Kristián of Eggenberg, Josef Adam of Schwarzenberg

If we return the same way to the 1st courtyard, directly opposite the gate we see another part of the former baroque fortification walls and linking on to them the former **baroque coach-house**, used today as a garage. Going alongside these structures in the direction of the little park, we come

The château lapidary with displays of the château's original sculptural decorations

on the right-hand side to the entrance to the basement of the former New Burgrave's House. Here we find one of the largest and most extensive Renaissance cellars in the Czech Republic (48 metres long) which served as stables and could accommodate up to 100 horses. There was a storehouse for beer here later, and in the 19th century a prison with walls neighboring the bear pit. The cellar was restored and today houses a remarkable **exhibition of manorial lapidary**, including the original sculptures from the château area and gardens. In order to protect them, they were restored and placed in the lapidarium exhibition, and copies made to put in the grounds. Coming out of the lapidarium, a small slope takes us back to the 1st courtyard to the main path leading to the château, and here we face the **Old Burgrave's House (No. 58)** where the burgrave, the highest officer and custodian of the castle, lived together with the scrivener or the tax-collector.

The Krumlov bears

Then on the right-hand side there are two **bastions** dating back to 1620 and a bridge across the bear pit. The bastions, which are part of the defence system built at the beginning of the Thirty Years War, are a memorial to Ferdinand Carrati de Carrara, who was commander of the castle garrison in 1620. Terracotta vases adorn the bastions as well as the figures of two lions bearing the family emblems, on the left that of Josef Adam of Schwarzenberg, and on the right that of his wife, Marie Theresia of Liechtenstein.

Not far away, on the stone bridge spanning the ditch there are further reminders of Josef Adam and his wife in the form of statues of St. Joseph, the Infant Jesus and the Virgin Mary (by Jan Antonín Zinner, 1759), symbolizing the married couple. From the bridge we get a good view of both parts of the **bear pit,** which was once part of the defence system of the Gothic castle. There was originally a wooden drawbridge here that prevented entrance to the castle through the 2nd courtyard. In 1999 the pit underwent reconstruction to make conditions there correspond with the natural surroundings to which the bears kept there are accustomed. The keeping of bears here is an old Rožmberk tradition.

The breeding of bears at the château began in the 16th century under the rule of the last Rožmberks. According to a family legend the Rožmberks were related to the old Italian House of Orsini. "Orsa" means a female bear and this motif was used by the last Rožmberks to illustrate their relationship to the Orsini family. It appears in their coat-of-arms as two bears bearing shields.

The bridge over the bear pit takes us to the entrance to the 2nd courtyard. The portal is decorated with three stone emblems, the Eggenberg (Jan Antonín of Eggenberg), Brandenburg (Marie Anna of Brandenburg) and the Rožmberk (William of Rožmberk) emblems. These same emblems are found in various forms on the façades and inside the château. The oldest building on

The castle moat with the enclosure for the bears

the 2nd courtyard is Little Castle (Hrádek) with the round tower. It was here on a rocky outcrop overlooking the River Vltava that the oldest early Gothic castle arose, consisting of a residential palace and a "refugee tower" that was not so high as that of today. From the foot of the rocks in the bear pit to the weathercock on top of the tower it measures 70.43 meters.

Little Castle (Hrádek) and the tower were given a new appearance particularly in the second half of the 16th century under William of Rožmberk. During that time the Italian architect, Baldassare Maggi of Arogna, gave it its Renaissance character with a wealth of mural paintings on the façades. The author of the fresco paintings was the local artist Bartoloměj Beránek-Jelínek. At that time the tower had bells (two of them were from the original Gothic tower), a timepiece and gongs; the biggest bell was cast by the famous Prague bell-founder Brikcí of Cimperk. As the years went by, the Little Castle and its tower gradually lost their Renaissance splendour and, marked by the ravages of time, it seemed that the grey shabby façades had forgotten their once multicoloured beauty. Little Castle then began to be used as storehouse, offices or dwelling for the château personnel, and gradually fell into disuse. From 1760 onwards it was occupied only by the watchman who wound up the clock, rang the bells and later announced the hour from the gallery by means of a trumpet. Renovation work was done on the Little Castle building and château tower in the 19th and 20th centuries with a certain amount

A view of the 2nd courtyard from the tower

The 2nd courtyard – the New Burgraviate

of success and the original Renaissance ornamental decoration of the façades was renewed so that Český Krumlov once again had its unique picturesque dominant feature. Today the tower is one of the most popular attractions for visitors; its gallery provides a glorious view of the town and château architecture, set against surroundings dominated by Blanský Forest (Blanský les) and Mount Kleť.

The **2nd courtyard** for a long time had the word "guard" attached to its name, derived from the members of the Schwarzenberg grenadier guards. They existed from 1742 to 1948 and were quartered on the ground floor of the New Burgrave's House (No. 59) standing to the right of the passage from the 1st courtyard. The number of guards was not stable; sometimes there were as many as 24 of them. They represented the Schwarzenberg family, guarded the courtyard and château tower, accompanied the manorial treasury on journeys, escorted criminals, played in the manorial band during manorial celebrations, and also helped with work on the farm and in the offices. We are reminded of them today by four canons standing in front of the building.

The New Burgrave's House is linked to the Little Castle. Its two wings occupy almost the entire east and north sides of the 2nd courtyard. It was also built by Baldassare Maggi of Arogna. The painting of the façades, in contrast to the colourful Little Castle and tower, was done in various shades of grey, using the chiaroscuro technique. It was the work of the painter, Gabriel de Blonde, or members of his workshop at the end of the 16th century. The murals of the New burgrave's house is one of the few examples in Central Europe showing the use of chiaroscuro, and its importance is underlined by the fact that the European Union gave financial support for the renovation of those murals in 1998.

The ground floor and first floor of the building were the administrative offices; today the rooms above the passage contain the château library of around 40 000 volumes – fiction and non-fiction amassed over the centuries by all generations of its aristocratic owners. In 1800 an agricultural institute was opened on the first floor by the Schwarzenbergs as one of the first agricultural colleges in Bohemia. Today that part contains extensive archives belonging to the state regional archives. Beside the bar-

The 3rd château courtyard

racks of the Schwarzenberg guard there was a taproom from 1752, and from 1842 also a casino.

Opposite the New burgrave's residence there stands the baroque building of the **Mint (Mincovna)**. It arose evidently in the 1680s in the times of Jan Kristián of Eggenberg, was completed in 1693 by Jakub Maggi and was intended to mint Eggenberg coins. But a law issued by the Emperor in 1702 forbidding the minting of small coins prevented it from ever fulfilling this purpose. After a fire in 1729 another store was built on top and rooms and an office for the master of the hunt were created. A reminder of this is the stone-carved head of a stag with antlers above one of the entrances to the building. Other parts were turned into rooms and offices and today the building houses the central cash desk, lecture halls and exhibition rooms. The last building on the north side of the 2nd courtyard is the **Dairy (Máselnice)** with a Renaissance façade decorated with graffiti and a sundial. It stands near the way leading to the Upper Castle (Horní zámek) and the 3rd courtyard. In the Middle Ages entrance to the castle was hindered by the second castle moat. A Gothic tower with stairs was built there; it was remodelled later in Renaissance style and today forms the core of the dairy where butter and other products were made for the manorial kitchen. Today a restaurant occupies the ground floor and above is a gallery exhibiting contemporary art.

Along the main way we come to the **entrance**, its portal decorated with the em-

The 4th château courtyard

blem of William of Rožmberk from the 1570s and the emblems of Jan Antonín of Eggenberg and Anna Marie of Brandenburg from 1646. A steeply rising vaulted passage with a wooden floor, installed by William of Rožmberk in 1577 at the place where the ditch used to be, takes us to the 3rd courtyard at the Upper Castle.

The Upper Castle (Horní zámek), later named the Upper Château, is a complex of palatial buildings surrounding the 3rd and the 4th courtyards. Thanks to their size, they dominate the entire area and together with the château tower add the finishing touch to the magnificent panorama of Český Krumlov. The Upper Castle was gradually built over the centuries according to the requirements of its owners and became more and more a representative noble residence; therefore its disposition is exceedingly complicated. The different adaptations and alterations in the various buildings are still to be seen today. First of all, before starting to build in the first half of the 14th century, the difficult rocky terrain had to be prepared and levelled, especially since there were parts of the site of the present 4th courtyard that sloped steeply down. Thus there originated a three-tiered system of Gothic cellars spreading practically under the entire Upper Castle. Part of the cellars, called the **Wenceslas Cellars (Václavské sklepy)**, are open to the public; in the 1990s they were converted into an art gallery. They got their name from the Czech king, Wenceslas (Václav) IV, who, the tradition goes, was twice imprisoned here by the Rožmberks at the turn of the 14th century. Access to this fantastic labyrinth of Gothic cellars is from the passage leading from the 4th courtyard on to the Clad Bridge (Plášťový most).

The Wenceslas cellars

A tour through the Upper Castle is a great attraction for visitors. Here they can go through the rooms inhabited by the lords of the castle in bygone days, where the Rožmberks, Eggenbergs and Schwarzenbergs dined, slept, studied and worked, where they rested, amused themselves, and practised various hobbies and artistic pursuits as well as partook in amorous adventures. They will see the chapels where they prayed, and places used by their guests, courtiers, officials and servants. Each room is furnished with period furniture corresponding more or less to the original arrangement, according to the lists and descriptions in the old inventories and to what had been preserved in the castle depositories.

After passing through the entrance from the passage between the 3rd and the 4th courtyards into the **vestibule**, a short baroque staircase takes us to the **Chapel of Saint George (kaple sv. Jiří)**. This was part of the original medieval castle from the very beginning and all the inhabitants of the castle, including the servants, attended services there. The first chapel was part of the castle standing on the site of the 2nd courtyard. When the Upper Castle arose, the chapel was transferred to that building and underwent several changes throughout the years. Its present aspect dates from 1750-1753 when the Viennese painter Mathias André decorated the walls with stucco in the rococo style. The statue of St. George above the altar is the work of Jan Antonín Zinner. The three altars of the chapel bear pictures: St. Anthony of Padua on the altar standing on the left-hand side, John of Nepomuk on the right-hand altar and the Virgin Mary with the infant Jesus on the main altar in the centre. They date from the time of the rococo changes and were repainted in the mid-19th century by the Schwarzenberg court painter, Charles Louis Philippot. A casket in the niche of the main altar contains the remains of St. Calixtus. Music always accompanied church services; in the chancel we can see a well-preserved organ, built in 1753 by Friedrich Ferdinand Semrád.

Leaving the chapel we go "back in time" to the Renaissance period, to the 1570s. In the passage leading to the various rooms we get an idea of how the Rožmberk castle looked around the year 1580. It is shown together with portraits of members of the House of Vitkovec on the famous picture called **"The Dividing of the Rose"**. On it the legendary "forefather Vítek" is shown dividing his property among his five sons and at the same time a five-petalled rose is added to the family coat-of-arms.

Before we enter the first room we can inspect two portraits hanging on the wall. They show the last Rožmberks – William and his younger brother, Petr Vok. **The Rožmberk Rooms** were renovated on the

The château chapel of Saint George

The 3rd Renaissance room with a richly decorative painting

orders of William, who was preparing to marry for the third time. He and his new wife, Anna Marie of Baden, then lived in these luxuriously furnished rooms with lovely decorated walls and coffered ceilings.

The most comprehensive picture of how a representative **Renaissance chamber** looked is presented by the best-preserved third room. The walls and ceilings are covered with paintings; the lowest part imitates decorative textiles. Above that are painted scenes from the Old Testament (e.g. Abraham sacrificing his son, Isaac, drunken Lot being tempted by his daughters, Joseph sold by his brothers into slavery) and from mythology (Bacchus, god of wine, and Ceres, goddess of fertility and crops). The murals date from 1577 and are the work of Gabriel de Blonde. The coffered ceiling is decorated with a five-petalled rose on each panel. A similar coffered ceiling but more richly ornamented is to be seen in **the fourth room**.

Here we can see a portrait of **Perchta of Rožmberk** who is associated with the Rožmberk White Lady. Perchta was married to Jan of Liechtenstein and had a very unhappy life with him. After her death in 1476 she began to haunt the Rožmberk castles in a flowing white robe and, it seems, performed good deeds. At night she soothed crying children and looked after Petr Vok to whom, when he reached maturity, she revealed a hidden treasure. This good spirit can be met with today, but you must take care what gloves she is wearing. Black gloves foretell bad news, like a misfortune, illness or penury; white gloves however bring news of future happiness, good health and love. But we now leave the

White Lady and rooms of the last Rožmberks and go up a baroque staircase to the second floor containing the Schwarzenberg apartment of the 1730s.

The first room, called the **Antechamber**, was the place where guests assembled before they were received by the host. The walls are hung with pictures of the former property of the Schwarzenbergs and Eggenbergs (Červený Dvůr Manor, the town of Graz, Gradiška Castle etc.), maps and two portraits by the Viennese painter Maxmilian Hannl, dating from 1730. They present the first Schwarzenberg couple to choose the Český Krumlov Château as their residence – Adam František of Schwarzenberg and his wife, Eleonora Amalie, nee of Lobkovitz. After the tragic death of Adam František in 1732 his widow lived in the apartment with her son Josef Adam.

Situated next to the Antecamera is the **Eggenberg Hall**, its walls hung with portraits of members of three generations of the Steiermark noble family of Eggenbergs, who owned the Krumlov estate from 1622 to 1713. The most notable object in the hall is the Gold Coach, displaying remarkable woodcarved ornamentation and gilding. It was built in Rome in 1638 by Giuseppe Fiochini, and was used in a ceremonial procession from Rome to Pope Urban VIII in the Vatican to inform him of the election of a new Emperor. Jan Antonín I of Eggenberg participated in that diplomatic mission. The coach was accompanied by the Eggenberg personal guards; one of their uniforms of black velvet ornamented with gold braid is displayed in a niche near the window.

Another of the rooms in the Schwarzenberg apartment is the **baroque dining room**, and here we can admire two magnificent tapestries. The mark BB reveals that they were woven in Brussels in Brabant province. The patterns for them were painted in 1616 by Peter Paul Rubens. These two tapestries represent the rich Schwarzenberg collection of 85 complete tapestries and two fragments which are stored partly in Český Krumlov and partly in Hluboká château. The collection is the largest of its kind in Bohemia and one of the richest in Europe.

After a festive banquet in the dining room, the noble guests could then move into

The Eggenberg Hall with its Golden Coach

The baroque dining room

the adjoining **Baldachin Salon**, where they could converse over a cup of coffee or play one of the board games (a backgammon board is exhibited here today). The walls of the salon, like the upholstery of the richly carved and gilded lounge suite, are crimson; the neighbouring bedroom is also in uniform tones of crimson.

The bed chamber of the lady of the château, where the main feature is the bed with a canopy, was in the 18th century also a place used for social activities. The

The baldaquin salon

small rooms or cabinets leading from it were used for various purposes. On the left is the so-called **Oriental Cabinet**, used for entertaining close friends. Its walls were decorated with oriental motifs in 1775 by František Jakub Prokyš. It has a rare chandelier of Meissen porcelain and an inlaid writing desk, which came from the famous workshop of David Roentgen. Adjoining the bed-chamber there is also a **dressing-room** where the lady's maid slept and a private chapel, also called the **Chapel of the Sick**.

Our next stop is the picture gallery and here we can examine paintings from the former Eggenberg and Schwarzenberg collections. The first definite written proof of the existence of the gallery dates back to 1733, when it contained 236 pictures and other objects, including furniture, because it served also as a grand living-room. The gallery was completely re-arranged in the 1980s and today presents the most valuable works of the château collection, particularly those by Flemish, Dutch, German and Italian masters.

Linked to the art gallery is the **Gentlemen's Salon** or study, furnished in the Biedermeier style dating from the time before the mid-19th century. Here what attracts the most attention is a collection of tobacco-pipes from the 18th to 19th centuries and made mainly of meerschaum. The pictures of some of the châteaux owned by the Schwarzenbergs from 1810 to 1830 are the work of the court painter Ferdinand Runk. One of them presents a picturesque view of people enjoying themselves on the frozen pond in Krumlov Park. Through the neighboring **Ladies' Salon** or boudoir and along the **Bavarian Gallery** we come to a staircase, which leads to the Hall of Mirrors.

The château picture gallery

The hall of mirrors

The **Hall of Mirrors (Zrcadlový sál)** was the place where magnificent baroque celebrations were held. Next to it is the Masquerade Hall, which is linked by the passage on the Clad Bridge (Plášťový most) to the royal box at the baroque theatre; from the theatre and the adjoining Renaissance house a covered passage leads to the château gardens. Thus the aristocratic guests could listen to a concert in the Hall of Mirrors, then if desired attend a fancy-dress ball in the Masquerade Hall, then

The Masquerade Hall

The Masquerade Hall, detail (Dottore)

attend a theatre performance and finally come out in the château park where the celebrations reached their peak with a magnificent fireworks display. The mural paintings in both halls and the theatre were done on the same principle of illusive painting, which in dim candlelight almost made the figures seem alive. The murals of the Hall of Mirrors were painted in 1768 by the Viennese artists Hans Wetschel and Leo Märkel; the decoration of the auditorium and scenery of the theatre is also their work. Large mirrors were set in the walls, hence the name the Hall of Mirrors. The floral motifs and musical instruments on its murals contrast with the variety of figural murals in the Masquerade Hall.

The Masquerade Hall (Maškarní sál) murals were painted in 1748 by Josef Lederer. Figures from the commedia dell'arte, aristocrats in fancy dress, Turks and Chinese, a comedian with a monkey dressed as Harlequin and so on decorate the walls. Guarding the entrance to the hall are two Schwarzenberg guardsmen in their typical off-white uniforms, with tall hats and sabres. The musicians were up on the balcony; it is as if they went away and left their instruments and scores hanging on the walls. Lederer also painted his own portrait drinking coffee and with a coffee pot bearing his name on the wall of one of the window recesses. The close relation between the painted figures and the reality of that period is borne out by the fact that many of the painted costumes and articles in the figures' hands were based on actual models which have been preserved in the château depositories to the present day. The Masquerade Hall illustrates the luxurious life style and ostentatious splendour of noble residences in the mid-18th century.

The Masquerade Hall, detail (Pantalon)

The salon of Princess Eleanor

Tour No. 2 of the castle shows us the somewhat more sober way of life of the aristocracy in the 19th century. First we visit the **Schwarzenberg Gallery** of family portraits. Then we enter the bedroom of the servant, who could be summoned to any part of the building by an ingenious system of bells arranged below the ceiling. A rod connected to one of the bells existed also in the neighboring **Music Salon**, which is furnished in the classicist style, and has a collection of the various musical

The parlour of Princess Eleanor

instruments played here, the most valuable of which is a Viennese piano (Hammerklavier). Our next stop is in the **bedroom of Princess Paulina** of Schwarzenberg, which features her portrait hanging above the sofa. A glance into the adjoining toilet gives visitors the opportunity to decide whether or not Paulina was right when she complained in her letters about the inadequate sanitary conditions at Český Krumlov Castle.

Passing through the next room, where other tapestries from the rich Schwarzenberg collections are displayed, then through the salon containing pictures by the court landscape painter, **Ferdinand Runk**, we go along the passage to the nine-room **suite of Jan Adolf of Schwarzenberg and his wife**, Eleonora, nee of Liechtenstein; the whole apartment is unique in that it presents an almost complete, authentic picture of the type of aristocratic dwelling in the second half of the 19th century. It was re-arranged according to the inventory of the year 1879 in which the furnishings of each room are described in great detail. The original furnishings were gradually found, restored and installed in their original place, and so today we can say that the present arrangement corresponds almost exactly to the reality of that period. First we enter the **Reception Room**, which has

The Clad Bridge (Plášťový most)

The machinery of the baroque theatre

The baroque theatre – the stage

upholstered furniture decorated with the Schwarzenberg and Liechtenstein coats of arms in appliqué as a reminder of the aristocratic couple who occupied the apartment. The next **salon** contains a life-size portrait of Princess Eleonora, painted by the Italian artist Mathias Schiavoni when the strikingly beautiful princess was 22 years old. From there we pass through the **Smoking Salon** with its remarkable display of tobacco-pipes and other items serving to enhance the enjoyment of smoking, such as special little caps and ornamented tobacco pouches. Next comes the **Reference Library** which served the needs of Jan Adolf, then the **Small Dining-Room** with a large number of European and Oriental decorative porcelain objects on the shelves,

A theatre box

in the sideboards and on the walls, and English pictures with hunting scenes, which were fashionable at that time.

From there we enter the private **rooms of Princess Eleonora – the Salon, Cabinet and bed chamber**, the walls of which are hung with tapestries from the Schwarzenberg collection. The rarest and loveliest tapestries from the "Aeneas and Dido" series, which were woven in Holland in 1620-1630 hang in the Cabinet that was her study. The bedchamber together with the dressing-room end our inspection of the Schwarzenberg suite.

From the castle rooms we go past the Wenceslas cellars on to the 5th courtyard. Our path takes us over the Clad Bridge (Plášťový most), bearing the statues of four saints; that of St. John of Nepomuk by the Český Krumlov sculptor, Jan Plansker, has been standing here since 1727, the other three, St. Felix of Cantalice, St. Václav and St. Anthony of Padua were modelled by a graduate of the Viennese Academy, sculptor Jan Antonín Zinner, about 20 years later.

On leaving the bridge we find ourselves standing in front of the **baroque theatre** on the 5th courtyard. The theatre is undoubtedly the most precious of all the ancient monuments at Český Krumlov Château. There exist only two theatres in the whole world where practically the entire original equipment from the second half of the 18th century has been preserved – one is at Drottningholm in Sweden, the other in Český Krumlov. Here in Český Krumlov almost 300 painted parts of stage scenery have been preserved, which enable the building of 13 basic sets with the possibility of several other variations. They include e. g. a Garden, Woods, a drawing room, an army camp, a prison, a festival hall and a church. Then there are nearly 600 pieces of the original theatre costumes and their accessories – gloves, stockings, shoes, helmets etc. Among them we can find the costume of a conjurer with the inevitable magic wand, musicians' costumes and so on. During performances there were many requisites, large and small (e. g. a doctor's syringe, shopkeeper's cart, sutler's wagon and so on), all of which are still to be seen today in the château depositories. We can also mention the extensive collection of original lighting equipment, machinery for producing sound effects, the technical apparatus and machinery of the auditorium and stage, the reversible music stand in the orchestra etc. Last but not least there is the enormous number of literary documents and repertoires filed in the local branch of the State Regional Archives or in the château library.

The winter hippodrome

The beginnings of the theatre date back to the 17th century. Jan Kristián of Eggenberg had the original theatre built in 1682. In 1766 Josef Adam of Schwarzenberg had the building improved and modernized. The interior decoration was done by the previously mentioned painters, Hans Wetschel and Leo Märkel, both from the school of the famous theatre architect, Giuseppe Galli Bibiena. An enormous wooden apparatus was built in the theatre, made up of an ingenious system of winches, pulleys, sliding frames, trap-doors, ropes etc., for operating the parts of the scenes as well as the curtain, footlights and sound-effects appliances. This machinery was the work of the carpenter Lorenzo Makho and served to quickly change the scenes during a performance. This could be done in about 10 to 12 seconds and had a most impressive effect on the audience. It took place in the dim light of candles and oil-lamps which partly revealed and partly concealed the various parts on the stage, thus stimulating the imagination of the audience, and erased the line dividing reality from illusion. As if by magic, before the eyes of the amazed spectators the scene of a harbour suddenly changed into an eerie deep forest which within several seconds could change into a château park, luxurious room or a miserable prison cell. To this was added a whole series of sound-effects imitating the patter of rain, rattle of a hailstorm, claps of thunder, the moaning of the wind or portentous howling of a gale, the familiar rattle of coach wheels and clatter of horse's hooves. This was perfectly combined with visual effects such as the imitation of waves breaking into white foam, the trap door enabling sudden disappearances or appearances, a flying apparatus permitting the dramatic arrival of a god, various lighting and firework effects and a bonfire.

Today extensive efforts are being made to conserve and restore this unique structure. The work is financed partly by the state and partly from the contributions of sponsors; the Baroque Theatre of Český Krumlov Fund plays an important role here. During the main tourist season when the number of performances is limited a tour of the theatre evokes for the visitors, at least partly, the atmosphere of the former glory of the theatre.

Back again in the real world after our visit to the theatre, we can now walk along the 5th courtyard, past the so-called **Renaissance House** and up a slope to the peaceful château gardens. The path going to the right takes us to the former **winter riding-school,** which is used today for holding cultural and social events. The riding-school was built in 1744-1746 in a Viennese rococo style, designed by Andreas Altomonte. It was used for exercising horses in winter or in bad weather when the summer riding-school on a terrace opposite could not be used. The stucco decoration above the entrance and on the eastern side of the building is the work of the Viennese sculptor Jan Antonín Zinner and the plasterer Matthias André. The winter riding-school is the only building in the whole château complex to have two identical chimneys.

The **château gardens** were laid out in a mannerist style after 1678 under Jan Kristián of Eggenberg. Over the following centuries they were re-designed several times according to the changes in styles and wishes of their aristocratic owners. The gardens were gradually renovated in the last three decades of the 20th century.

The whole garden is surrounded by a wall with openings permitting views of the countryside. It lies on sloping ground and is oblong-shaped, measuring roughly 150 by 750 metres. Almost 11 hectares of this area is divided into four terraces, the lowest lying of which (designated today as the Orchard) lies along the left-hand side of the path leading to the winter riding-school. On the oldest plans of the garden dating from the start of the 18th century this part was the private garden of the ducal family and was called the Royal Garden. Since 1686 it has had a passage over it starting from the west wing of the Upper Castle and ending near the **summer riding-school** on a higher level of the terrain. Horses were exercised here in the past and in 1746 there was also a skittle-alley, which no longer exists.

Steps leading from the summer riding-school take us to what is called the **Lower Parterre of the gardens**. Shaped roughly in a square, it is symmetrically laid out and after reconstruction work carried out from 1969 to 1978 evokes the appearance of the original rococo gardens. The dominant feature of the slope dividing the Lower Parterre and the higher-placed Upper

The fountain in the château garden

An aerial view of the château garden

The Bellarie Summerhouse

Garden is the **cascade fountain** – one of the most beautiful and most valuable in the Czech lands. Its construction began after 1750 and was designed by the Viennese architect Andreas Altomonte and probably also by Jan Antonín Zinner. It was evidently modelled on the somewhat older, richly sculptured fountains in the gardens of the Belvedere Palace in Vienna. The four-tiered cascade fountain is decorated with a trio of water gods and nymphs, fish and frogs, an ornamental balustrade, 20 decorative vases and allegories of the four seasons of the year. The sculptures are of limestone and are the work of Matyáš Griessler, supervised and aided by Jan Antonín Zinner. From 1781 goldfish were kept in the fountain. Between 1996 and 1998 the fountain underwent renovation when the main sculptures were replaced by copies, partly financed by the World Monuments Fund. The original statues are now to be seen in the Château Lapidarium.

There, where the Lower Parterre reaches the Upper Garden, a path leads up to the main axis of the garden. That road connects the main gateway to the garden with the former garden gateway in the opposite wall, where a small house was built at the end of the 17th century for the gatekeeper. Today it is a fashionable public house with a large fireplace.

The Upper Garden, measuring 150 by over 500 metres, is the most extensive of the terraces in the Český Krumlov gardens. In contrast to the symmetrical layout of the Lower Parterre, most of it is styled like an English park, with some parts having the character of woods. Nevertheless the baroque style is still recognisable from the disposition of the paths and the preserved buildings. At first glance the object that attracts our attention is the modern construction of the **revolving auditorium** which enables visitors to enjoy on summer nights the remarkable experience of an open-air theatre show. The originator of the idea for such an auditorium and founder of the famous tradition of Český Krumlov open-air theatre performances was the architect Joan Brehms in the 1950s. At present the suitability of having this technical achievement in the centre of the historical château gardens is being debated.

On the right-hand side of the auditorium we see the **Bellarie Summerhouse**, one of the most priceless buildings in Bo-

The pond in the château garden

hemia. The original pavilion stood here already in 1692. Under the Eggenbergs it underwent several changes until in the latter half of the 18th century Andreas Altomonte converted it into the rococo style and so it has remained till today. On the storey above, the painter created mural pictures of illusive architecture, supplemented by vases, festoons and groups of cupids.

František Jakub Prokyš is also the creator of the decoration in the nearby **Music Pavilion** dating from 1752. He painted allegories of the seasons of the year on the ceiling, and what is remarkable is that although inadequately protected against weather conditions, they have survived nearly 250 years practically without any great damage. Unfortunately the destructive activities of some visitors/vandals are a bigger threat to the pavilion; perhaps only the former maze of hornbeams surrounding the pavilion from 1752 to 1843 could prevent their vandalism.

Our journey continues past clumps of trees to the **château pond**, square in shape and situated in the highest part of the gardens. In the middle of the pond is a small island in the centre of which there was once a pool with a jet of water shooting out of it. Swans were kept at the pond as early as in 1731 and in the same year a porpoise could be seen there, albeit only a wooden model on a metal pedestal. The surface of the pond is covered with lovely water lilies, which emphasize the romantic atmosphere of this corner.

The garden wall behind the pond closes off the extensive grounds of the château. All parts of the castle and château cannot be thoroughly inspected and appreciated on a single visit – that would require oceans of time. But even a short visit can leave us with a strong impression, a feeling that "history has breathed" on us and that beauty and romance have "spoken" to us. We can take all this with us from a visit to the castle and château of Český Krumlov – like a colourful reminder from an excursion, helping us to overcome the monotony of everyday life.

The Little Castle (Hrádek) with the château tower

ČESKÝ KRUMLOV - A HISTORICAL SUMMARY

6000–5000 B. C. the oldest Neolithic period settlement in the area
1253 the first written mention of Krumlov Castle
1274 the first written mention of the Old Town established on the opposite bank of the Vltava
1290 Záviš of Falkenštejn, the best-known member of the Krumlov branch of the House of Vitkovec, executed in front of Hluboká
1302 Krumlov became the seat of the House of Rožmberk after the Lords of Krumlov died out
1309 Krumlov was first mentioned as a town
1340 the construction of the Church of St. Vitas commenced
1350 the Minorite monastery was established
1394 Wenceslas (Václav) IV imprisoned at Krumlov Castle
1439 Krumlov first mentioned with the epithet "Český"
1520 the "Kaplanka" (Horní 159), the first Renaissance building in the town, was completed
1555 the Old Town and Latrán unified into a single urban unit
1586 the foundation stone was laid in the Jesuit hostel
1592 the Renaissance lord, William of Rožmberk, died
1598 the town was in the grip of a plague epidemic
1601 the last Rožmberk, Petr Vok, was forced to sell Český Krumlov to Emperor Rudolf II
1611 the invasion of Krumlov by the troops of the bishop of Passau
1622 the House of Eggenberg acquired the Český Krumlov estates
1648 Swedish troops seized the city
1652 the Jesuit seminary in Upper Street (Horní ulice) (building number 152) was completed as the first baroque building in the town
1680 construction of the baroque château theatre commenced
1719 the House of Schwarzenberg gained the Český Krumlov estates
1766 the renovation of the baroque theatre into its current appearance
1773 the Jesuit hostel closed with the dissolution of the Jesuit order
1860 the Schönbauer workshop began the traditional production of mouldings and frames in the town
1890 the photographic studio of Josef Seidl was established
1892 the České Budějovice – Český Krumlov – Kájov – Želnava railway line began operation
1906 electrification of the town commenced
1920 Krumlov was officially renamed Český Krumlov
1938 part of Český Krumlov was annexed by the Third Reich
1945 the liberation of Český Krumlov by the American army
1950 the château became the property of the Czechoslovak Republic
1958 the rotating auditorium began its activities with its first theatrical performance
1963 Český Krumlov declared an urban conservation area
1968 the 1st year of the annual Celebrations of the Five-Petalled Rose
1989 the grounds of castle and château were declared a national cultural monument
1992 Český Krumlov was entered in the UNESCO world heritage list

www.eggenberg.cz
Eggenberg
1560
PIVOVAR ČESKÝ KRUMLOV
RESTAURANT
BREWERY - BEERHOUSE EGGENBERG
Český Krumlov
established 1560

SIGNIFICANT PERSONALITIES

Altomonte, Andreas (1699-1780), architect, among other things, designed the château gardens and riding hall

d'Austria, don Julius Caesar (probably 1586-1609), illegitimate son of emperor Rudolf II, lived in Krumlov, insane murderer of the daughter of the local barber

Balbín, Bohuslav (1621-1688), scholar, author of the patriotic *Protection of Slavic Languages and in Particular Czech* (Obrana jazyka slovanského, zvláště pak českého), taught at the Jesuit seminary

Beránek, known as Jelínek, Bartoloměj († 1618), Rožmberk court painter, the Renaissance fresco decoration of the tower and the castle

Brehms, Joan (1907-1995), theatre architect, set designer, designed the theatre with the revolving stage

Březan, Václav (1568-1618), Rožmberk chronicler and librarian, author of the *History of the Rožmberks*

de Blonde, Gabriel († 1581), painter, the fresco decoration of the façade on the third courtyard and further château areas

Cometta of Eckthurn, Dominico Benedetto († about 1620), Renaissance architect, amongst other things the builder of the Budějovice Gate, the Church of St. Jošt and the town brewery

of Eggenberg, Jan Kristián I (1641-1710), baroque aristocrat, had built the baroque theatre, the new château garden and the mint among other things

of Falkenštejn, Záviš (about 1250-1290), aristocrat, member of the Krumlov branch of the House of Vitkovec, husband to Queen Kunhuta, the widow of Premyslid Otakar II, executed in front of Hluboká

Kelly, Edward (1565-1594), alchemist, active in the court of Emperor Rudolf II, later in the service of William of Rožmberk

Krčín of Jelčan, Jakub (1535-1604), Rožmberk regent and fishpond manager, fishpond builder

Lederer, Josef (18th century), rococo painter, painted the decorations in the Masquerade Hall (Maškarní sál)

Wenceslas IV of Luxembourg (1361-1419), Holy Roman Emperor and Czech King, imprisoned for a short time in Český Krumlov castle

Maggi of Arogno, Baldassare (about 1550-1619), Renaissance architect and builder, renovated the château tower and built the Jesuit hostel amongst other things

Maggi, Jakub († 1706), builder, the baroque renovation of the château and the Minorite monastery amongst other things

Matyáš Habsburg (1557-1619), Holy Roman Emperor and Czech King, owned the Krumlov estates from 1602, visited Krumlov on several occasions

Porák, Arnošt († 1918), industrialist, developed the paper industry and graphite mining

Prokyš, František Jakub (1713-1791), baroque and rococo painter, decorated the Bellarie Summerhouse and a number of areas within the château and its environs

of Rožmberk, Jindřich III († 1412), aristocrat, the highest burgrave of the Czech Kingdom

of Rožmberk, Perchta (about 1429-1476), aristocrat, according to legend she appeared as a white ghost after her death

of Rožmberk, Petr IV (1462-1523), aristocrat, the county sheriff, the Renaissance renovation of the castle began under his reign

of Rožmberk, William (1535-1592), aristocrat, diplomat, politician, bearer of the Order of the Golden Fleece, renovated the castle into a Renaissance residence

Seidel, Josef (1859-1935), photographer, had his own company and photographic studio in Český Krumlov

Schiele, Egon (1890-1918), painter, stayed in Český Krumlov, painted the town and the local inhabitants

of Schwarzenberg, Josef Adam (1722-1782), aristocrat, undertook the baroque renovation of the chateau, established the château theatre and the Masquerade Hall

of Schwarzenberg, Karel I Filip (1771-1820), aristocrat, diplomat, field marshal, defeated Napoleon at Leipzig (1813)

EGON SCHIELE ART CENTRUM

ČESKÝ KRUMLOV

© Libor Sváček

The Egon Schiele Art Centrum mainly offers classic 20th century art, changing exhibitions of contemporary art, spacious international studios for residential stays of artists, a large museum shop and a café in the architecturally superb premises of a 16th century former Municipal Brewery over an exhibition area of more than 4000 square metres.

© Manfred Schöller

www.schieleartcentrum.cz

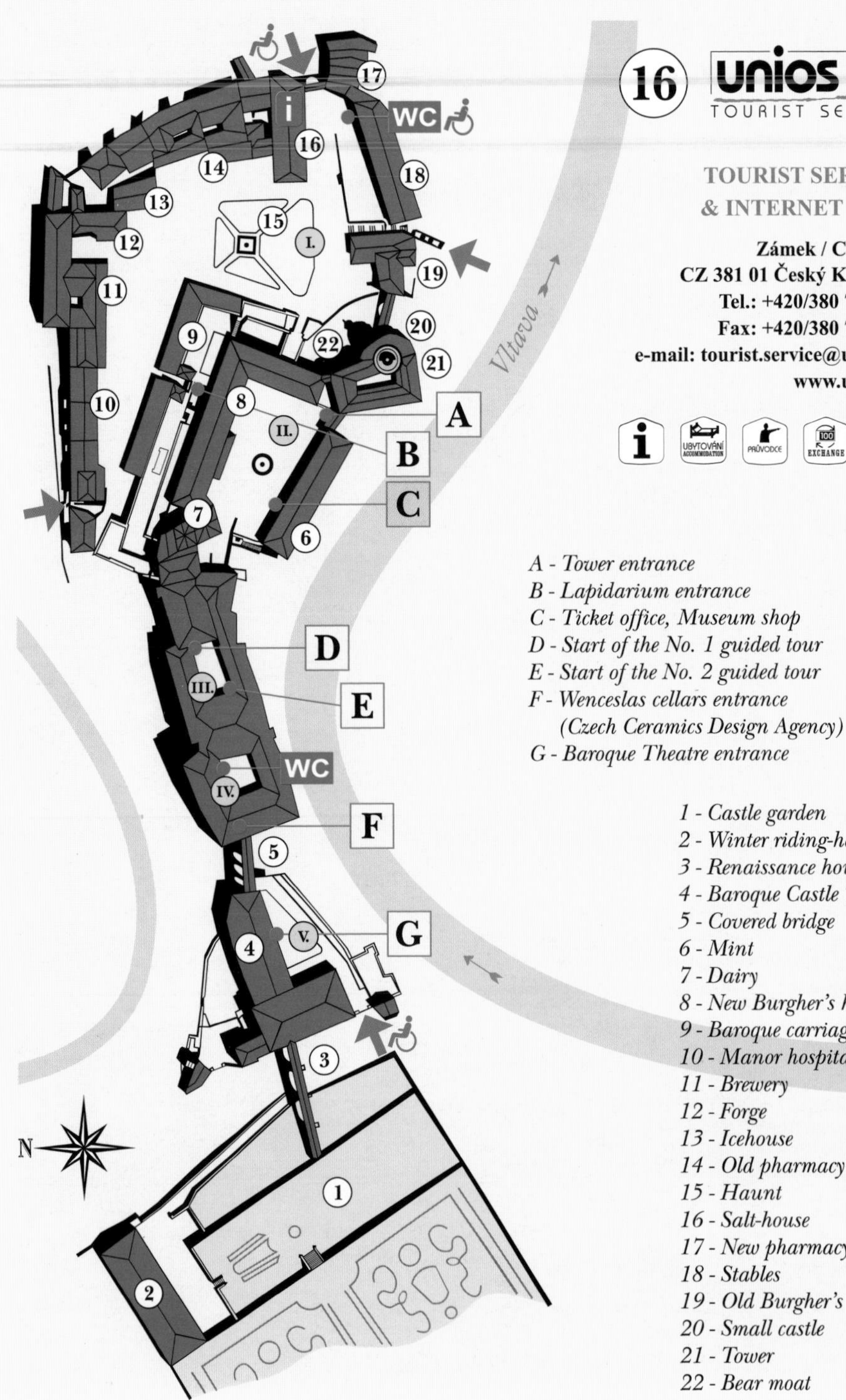

16 

TOURIST SERVICE
& INTERNET CAFÉ

Zámek / Castle 57
CZ 381 01 Český Krumlov
Tel.: +420/380 712 219
Fax: +420/380 712 424
e-mail: tourist.service@unios.cz
www.unios.cz

A - Tower entrance
B - Lapidarium entrance
C - Ticket office, Museum shop
D - Start of the No. 1 guided tour
E - Start of the No. 2 guided tour
F - Wenceslas cellars entrance
(Czech Ceramics Design Agency)
G - Baroque Theatre entrance

1 - Castle garden
2 - Winter riding-hall
3 - Renaissance house
4 - Baroque Castle Theatre
5 - Covered bridge
6 - Mint
7 - Dairy
8 - New Burgher's house
9 - Baroque carriage halls
10 - Manor hospital
11 - Brewery
12 - Forge
13 - Icehouse
14 - Old pharmacy
15 - Haunt
16 - Salt-house
17 - New pharmacy
18 - Stables
19 - Old Burgher's house
20 - Small castle
21 - Tower
22 - Bear moat

mezinárodní hudební festival
international music festival
český krumlov
Hlavní pořadatel
Main organiser
Auviex s.r.o.
Perlitová 1820, 140 00 Praha 4
Česká republika
tel.: +420 241 445 404
fax: +420 241 445 584
auviex@auviex.cz
www.czechmusicfestival.com
Předprodej vstupenek
Advance ticket sales
Infocentrum Český Krumlov
Nám. Svornosti 2
381 01 Český Krumlov
tel.: +420 380 704 621
fax: +420 380 704 619
infocentrum@ckrf.ckrumlov.cz
Unios Tourist Service
Zámek 57 - Solnice
381 01 Český Krumlov
tel.: +420 380 725 110
fax: +420 380 712 424
tourist.service@unios.cz

TRAVELLER'S HOSTEL

Travellers' Hostel
Soukenická 43, 381 01 Český Krumlov
Tel./Fax: +420 - 380 711 345
e-mail: krumlov@travellers.cz
www.travellers.cz

Travellers' Hostel - Accommodation in the town centre. Prices start at 270 CZK/person/night with breakfast, 4-8 bed rooms, 1 suite. A bar with a great atmosphere, billiards, football and live music. Internet access and laundry service available.

Pension Vltava
Kájovská 62, 381 01 Český Krumlov,
tel./fax: +420-380 711 978
e-mail: ckvltava@ckvltava.cz,
www.ckvltava.cz

Pension Vltava is situated in the old town centre in a historical building dating from the 15th century. In 1996 it was reconstructed. It offers accommodation with breakfast in 2-, 3- or 4-bed bedrooms with their own bathrooms and toilets. Parking spaces are right next to the house.

Hotel U města Vídně
Latrán 77, 381 01 Český Krumlov
Tel.: +420-380 720 111, Fax: +420-380 720 119
e-mail: info@hmv.cz, www.hmv.cz

A romantic, carefully renovated hotel in the historical centre of Český Krumlov, right in the heart of a UNESCO cultural heritage site. After a planned reconstruction and another expansion (Residence Latrán) in autumn 2004, the hotel represents a new quality dimension in hotel services in Český Krumlov. It is located only 100 m away from the castle and a 3 minute walk to all the major tourist attractions in Český Krumlov.

Zapa Bar
Latrán 15, 381 01 Český Krumlov
tel.: +420/380 712 559
barzapa@quick.cz

- *a choice of 150 kinds of mixed drinks*
- *wide choice of liqueurs and spirits from all over the world*
- *open daily 6 p.m.–1 a.m.*

ČESKÝ KRUMLOV

THE OFFICIAL TOURIST INFORMATION CENTRE FOR THE TOWN

Comprehensive services & current information about the offer and cultural events in Český Krumlov and its surroundings.

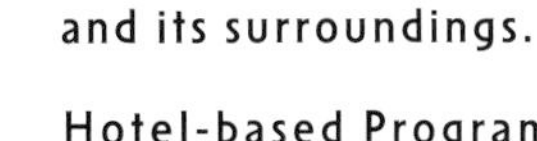

Hotel-based Programmes.

Attractive stays and trips for groups and individuals.
Special offers, including **The Best of Český Krumlov.**

Accommodation Services.

Over 100 selected partners. Recommendation and accommodation booking in hotels, B&Bs and private rooms.

Guide Services

Professional guides for groups (8 world languages).
AudioGuide - a pocket guide, 60 minutes of history, legends and numerous objects of interest.

Tickets and Map Centre.
Internet. Exchange office. Left luggage office.
Issue of ISIC and IYTC cards.
Car rental. Sale of fishing licences.
DHL delivery service reception.

INFOCENTRUM. YOUR PARTNER 365 DAYS A YEAR.

Náměstí Svornosti 2, 381 01 Český Krumlov
Tel.: +420/ 380 704 622-3 • Fax: +420/ 380 704 619
e-mail: infocentrum@ckrf.ckrumlov.cz • www.ckrumlov.cz/infocentrum

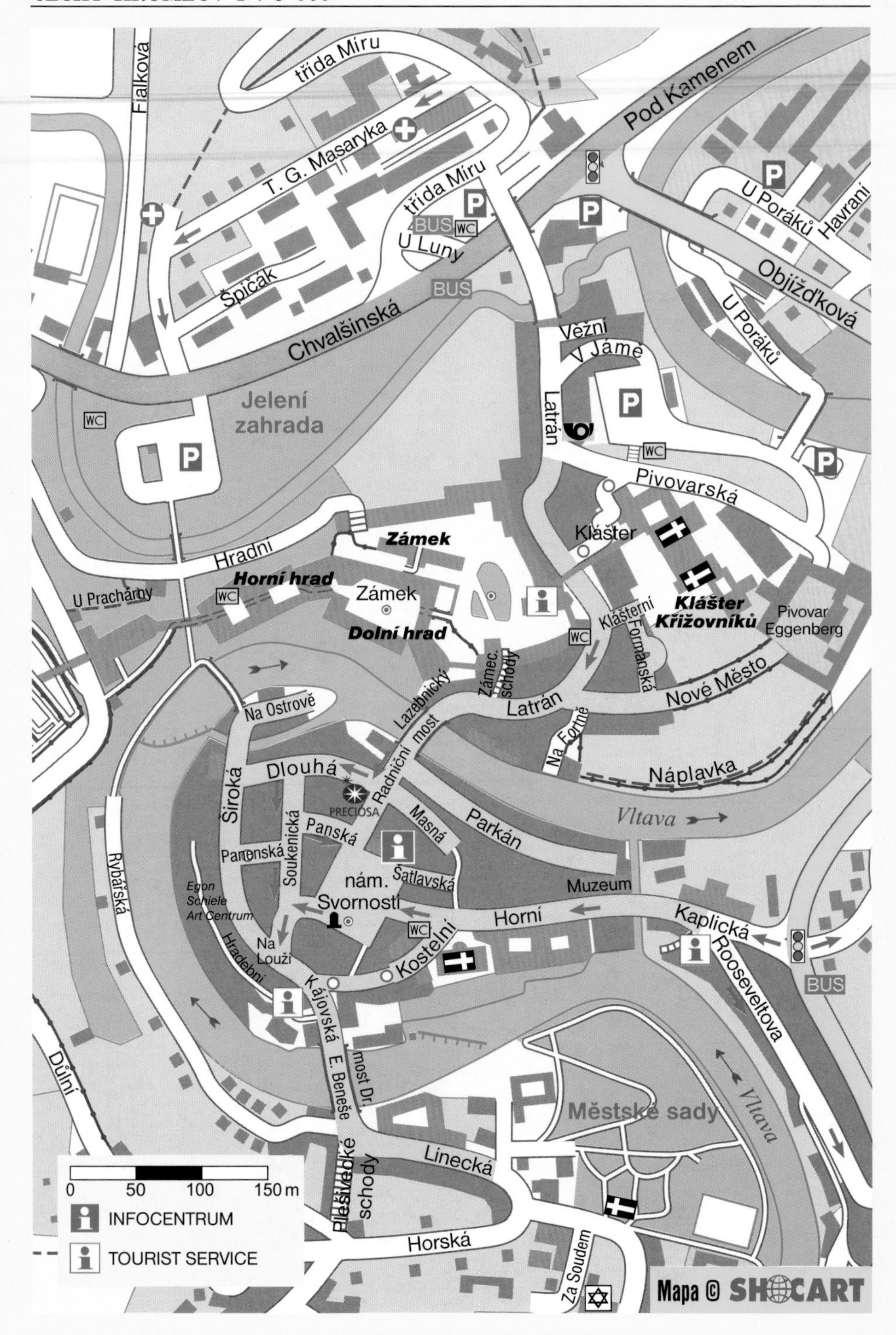

Fialková
třída Míru
T. G. Masaryka
Pod Kamenem
třída Míru
BUS
WC
U Luny
U Poráků
Havraní
Objížďková
U Poráků
Špičák
BUS
Chvalšinská
Vězní
V Jámě
Latrán
WC
Jelení
zahrada
WC
Pivovarská
Klášter
Zámek
Hradní
Horní hrad
U Prachárny
WC
Zámek
Klášter
Křižovníků
Pivovar
Eggenberg
Dolní hrad
Klášterní
Formánská
WC
Zámec. schody
Lazebnický most
Nové Město
Latrán
Na Ostrově
Na Fortně
Náplavka
Dlouhá
Radniční
PRECIOSA
Široká
Soukenická
Panská
Masná
Parkán
Vltava
Panenská
Egon
Schiele
Art Centrum
nám.
Svornosti
Šatlavská
Muzeum
Horní
Kaplická
WC
Rybářská
Hradební
Na Louži
Kostelní
Rooseveltova
Kájovská
BUS
Dlouhá
most Dr. E. Beneše
Městské sady
Vltava
Linecká
Plešivecké schody
Horská
Za Soudem
0
50
100
150 m
INFOCENTRUM
TOURIST SERVICE
Mapa © SHOCART